Date Due

| | | | |
|---|---|---|---|
| OCT 9 1982 | | | |
| DEC 1 8 1982 | | | |
| MAR 1 4 199 | MAR 2 7 2001 | | |
| MAY 2 1 | JUN 2 7 2001 | | |
| JAN 1 9 1998 | APR 2 5 2004 | | |
| JUL 5 1999 | | | |
| MAY 7 1998 | | | |
| NOV 8 1993 | | | |
| NOV 0 9 1994 | | | |
| MAR 0 2 1995 | | | |

# LAND TRAVEL
# from the Beginning

*by Alma Gilleo*
*illustrated by John Nelson*

ELGIN, ILLINOIS 60120


Distributed by Childrens Press, 1224 West Van Buren Street, Chicago, Illinois 60607.

**Library of Congress Cataloging in Publication Data**
Gilleo, Alma, 1920-
  Land travel from the beginning.
  SUMMARY: A history of land travel from walking to wagons to the sophisticated modes of travel in the present and projected for the future.
  1. Transportation—Juvenile literature. [1. Transportation] I. Nelson, John, 1928- II. Title.
TA1149.G54            629.04              77-24068
ISBN 0-89565-000-2

In early days, when people wanted to go from one place to another, they walked. It was the only way to travel. There were no cars and no trucks. There were no buses and no trains. There were no tame horses. There were not even any bicycles.

To move things from one place to another was hard. People carried things in their arms. They carried things on their shoulders. Sometimes they carried things on their heads. And sometimes they pushed and pulled things.

Travel was slow. And moving things was hard work.

Then someone thought of an easier way to move things. He tied logs together. On top of the logs, he put what he wanted to move. Then he pulled the logs along the ground, like a sled.

This first sled was called a sledge. It was hard work to pull a heavy sledge. But it was easier than carrying a heavy load.

Later, men made a sledge with two logs on the bottom. This sledge was still easier to pull.

Then some smart man trained a dog to pull a sledge. And in the North, people taught reindeer to pull sledges over snow and ice. Now people had pets, and their work was easier too.

4

But people still needed to learn how to move very heavy things, such as huge rocks.

"Let's try something new," someone said. With friends to help, he put logs under a sledge. The men pulled the sledge forward. The logs rolled. The sledge moved easily.

As the sledge moved forward, it rolled off the back log. Someone picked up that log and moved it to the front. Over and over, he had to move the logs, as the sledge was pulled.

This was hard work. But it wasn't as hard as pushing a giant rock.

"Logs roll," someone said. "A slice of a log will roll too." He cut a slice of a log. He tried it. It rolled. He had a wheel.

No one knows for sure who invented the first wheel. But it was an important invention. Men soon learned to put a piece of wood between two wheels to make a cart.

By this time, people had tamed oxen. Men used the strong oxen to pull their carts. Now people could move heavy loads easily. They could ride in their carts too.

Men soon learned to make thinner wheels. Some had spokes of wood. These spokes were like the ones in the picture at the top of the next page.

Later, men learned to tame wild horses. Think how wonderful it must have been, to tame a wild horse! To ride him! To teach him to pull something!

One of the first ways men used horses was to pull war chariots. The big picture shows a war chariot. It has thinner wheels with metal spokes. These wheels were lighter than those made of wood. They could turn faster and easier.

Horses could travel faster than oxen. Now soldiers could travel to faraway cities in their fast chariots.

Mesopotamian Cart
Assyrian Chariot

After that, it was a long time before men made still better vehicles for travel. But during that time, they did something else that helped travel. They made roads!

China had good roads at an early date. So did Rome. Roads were made in many other countries. People could travel in carts and wagons on the new roads.

Someone put a roof over a four-wheeled cart. Rich people often rode in this kind of cart.

In the early days of America, many people traveled in covered wagons. Later, the buggy was invented. The picture at the bottom of the page shows a buggy called a one-horse shay.

Covered Cart, 15th Century
Prairie Schooner
One-Horse Shay

People kept looking for ways to make travel faster. They kept looking for ways to make work easier. About this time, someone built a new machine. This machine pumped water out of mines. Soon it did other work too. It was called a steam engine. It used the steam from boiling water to make power.

A man in England made a small steam engine and put it on a carriage. His carriage moved by engine power instead of by horse power.

Later, men made better steam engines. Some were used to run small buses in London. Many people were afraid of steam engines, though, so they were not used long.

The picture shows one of the first steam carriages.

Can you find the steam engine? It is in back.

The man who made the first steam carriage had another idea. He made a steam locomotive. It ran on tracks. It went four or five miles an hour.

Other men made steam locomotives that could travel faster. They were first used to pull cars of coal from the coal mines.

The steam locomotive was called an iron horse. Can you guess why? It took the place of the horse. It could run faster than a horse. It could pull heavier loads too. Sometimes, people on horses would race steam locomotives. They wanted to beat the trains. But they couldn't.

Steam locomotives pulled trains in America and in other countries. A train ride was fast and comfortable. But people were still trying to find new ways to travel.

16

Another vehicle for travel was invented in Europe. It was the bicycle.

You would have thought the first bicycle was funny. There was no way to steer it. It did not have any pedals. To ride it, a person sat on the seat. He pushed on the ground with his feet. It was like walking or running while sitting on a bicycle. A picture of this walking bicycle is at the top of the next page.

A long time later, someone found a way to steer the bicycle. Someone else made pedals for it. Then people made many kinds of bicycles.

On the next page, there is a picture of a man riding one of the early bicycles. This bicycle is called the High Bicycle. Would you like to ride on a bicycle that high?

18

Early Bicycle
—the Draisine
High-Wheeler

You know about bicycles. You may even have one. You also know about buses. Did you know that the first bus was pulled by horses? It was.

Paris had the first buses. Each bus was a carriage pulled by two horses. Seven people could ride in the first bus. Soon, people made larger buses. These were pulled by four horses. Many cities used these buses.

Tramways were used in cities too. A tram was like a railroad car. It ran on tracks, but it was pulled by one or two horses.

These trams were called horse cars or streetcars. Look at the picture of the horse car on the next page. Wouldn't you like to ride in one?

Transportation was changing quickly. One of the most important changes came when a new engine was made in France. Its power came from gasoline.

Soon this new engine was used on small cars in Germany. The cars were called automobiles.

In America, Henry Ford became famous, making automobiles. His first car was made in 1903.

Many people wanted to buy his cars. Ford couldn't keep up with the orders. Then he invented a way to make cars more quickly. Soon his factory made 100 cars a day.

The pictures on the next page show some of the early cars. Which one do you like best? Do you know anyone who has an old car? How are the old cars different from today's cars?

Ford Quadricycle
1903 Ford Model A
1914 Dodge

The first cars didn't travel very fast. It was just as well, because roads were not always smooth and easy to travel. They were not like the ones in the picture.

Dirt roads had deep ruts. In dry weather, they were so dusty they made people cough. In wet weather, oh, were they muddy! Even gravel roads were dusty and bumpy.

Tar was first used to make a smooth road in the tiny country of Monaco. The first concrete road was made in Detroit soon after cars were invented.

Today, good roads are found in many parts of the world. Many different kinds of vehicles travel the super highways. How many kinds do you see in the picture?

24

As roads changed and cars changed, trains changed too. More than 50 years ago, a Diesel-electric engine was made in France. It could travel faster than the steam locomotive. Soon it was used on trains around the world. For years, many people traveled on this kind of train. In some countries, they still do.

But, in America today, not many people like to travel this way. Some people drive their cars to faraway cities. Other people would rather fly.

Some people, however, do take fast Diesel-electric trains to work every day. And a few trains still carry people between cities. But the Diesels are used now mostly for carrying things.

Today there are many ways to travel by land. People have even traveled on the land surface of the moon. On the next page is a picture of a lunar rover. It was taken to the moon aboard the Apollo 15 spacecraft. It gets its power from batteries.

Men drove the rover to explore the moon. They didn't drive far—just 17 miles. But without the rover, they could not have carried rocks back to the spacecraft. On earth, scientists studied the rocks and learned much about the moon.

The rover is still parked on the moon. It shows us that people can make new ways to travel when they are needed.

One of the newest ways to travel is by monorail. A monorail is a railroad. It is different from railroads you see in your town. The monorail runs on only one track. That track is high off the ground. There are two kinds of monorails. On one kind, the train travels on top of a large rail. On the other kind, the train hangs below the rail. A ride on a monorail is fast and smooth.

Monorails are found in only a few cities. Maybe someday there will be more of them. The picture shows what monorails might look like in the future.

What do you think travel will be like in the future?

Probably cars will be smaller than the ones we have today. Smaller cars should use less gas. That is important, because the world is running out of oil. (Gas is made from oil.)

Many years ago, an electric car was invented. It could travel only a short distance. Now people are trying to make a better electric car.

People are thinking of many new ideas for land travel. Trains that could speed through tubes is one idea.

Can you think of other ideas?